EASY GUITAR
WITH NOTES & TAB

ROCK SONGS FOR KIDS

ISBN 978-1-7051-4241-7

Visit Hal Leonard Online at
www.halleonard.com

Contact Us:
Hal Leonard
7777 West Bluemound Road
Milwaukee, WI 53213
Email: info@halleonard.com

In Europe, contact:
Hal Leonard Europe Limited
42 Wigmore Street
Marylebone, London, W1U 2RN
Email: info@halleonardeurope.com

In Australia, contact:
Hal Leonard Australia Pty. Ltd.
4 Lentara Court
Cheltenham, Victoria, 3192 Australia
Email: info@halleonard.com.au

Beat It

Words and Music by Michael Jackson

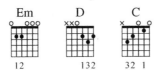

Strum Pattern: 1, 2
Pick Pattern: 2, 4

Intro
Moderately fast

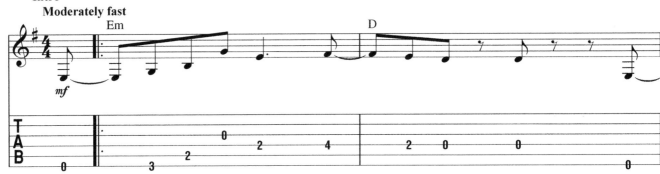

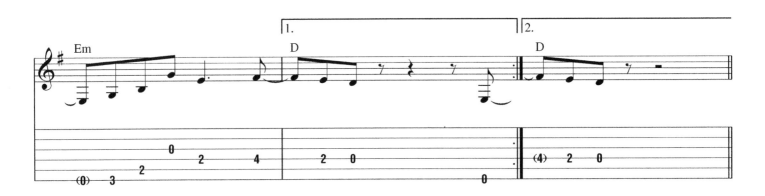

1. They told him, "Don't you ev - er come a - round here. Don't wan - na see your face; you bet - ter
2. *See additional lyrics*

dis - ap - pear." The fi - re's in their eyes and their words are real - ly clear. So

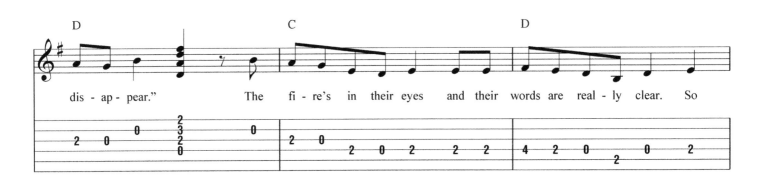

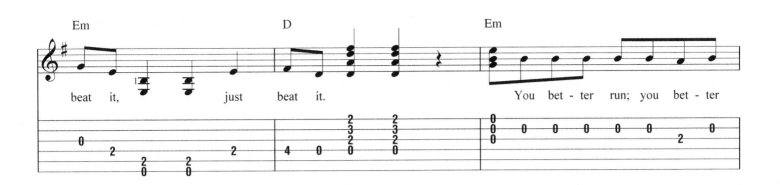

To Coda ⊕

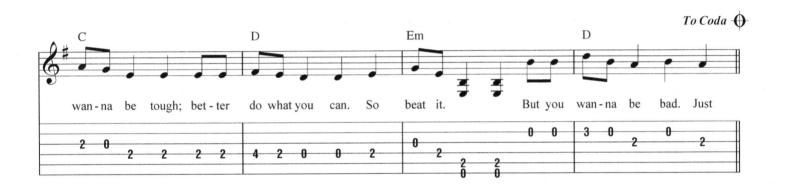

Chorus

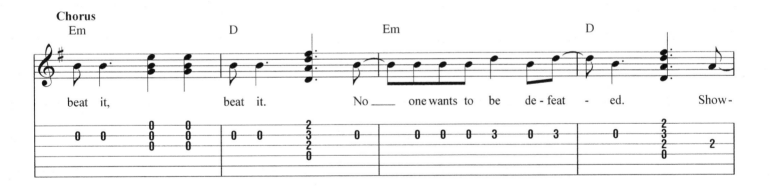

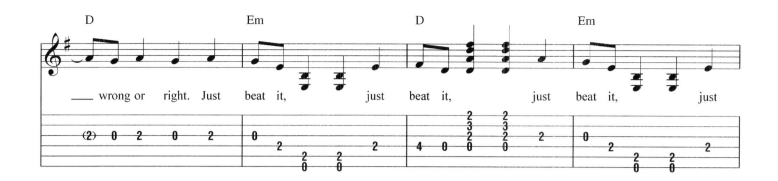

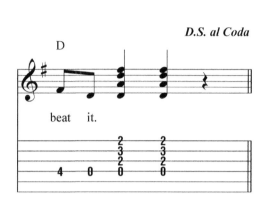 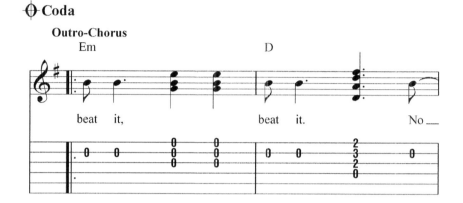

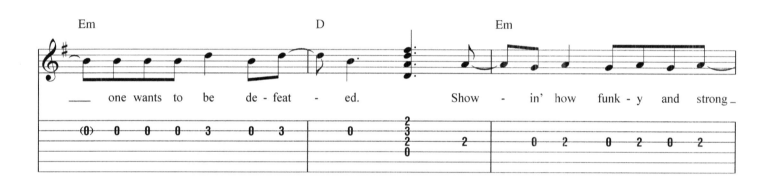

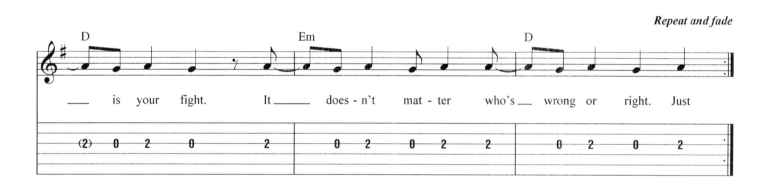

Additional Lyrics

2. They're out to get you, better leave while you can.
   Don't wanna be a boy, you wanna be a man.
   You wanna stay alive, better do what you can.
   So beat it, just beat it.
   You have to show them that you're not really scared.
   You're playin' with your life. This ain't no truth or dare.
   They'll kick you, then they beat you, then they'll tell you it's fair.
   So beat it. But you wanna be bad.

Crocodile Rock

Words and Music by Elton John and Bernie Taupin

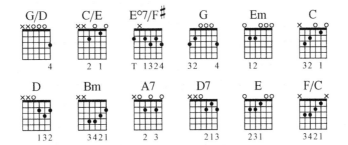

Strum Pattern: 3, 6
Pick Pattern: 4, 5

Intro
Moderately fast

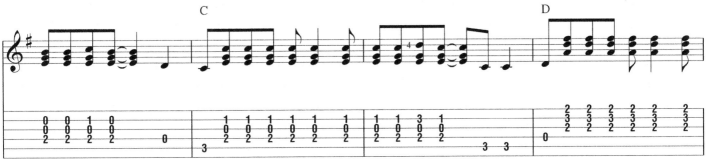

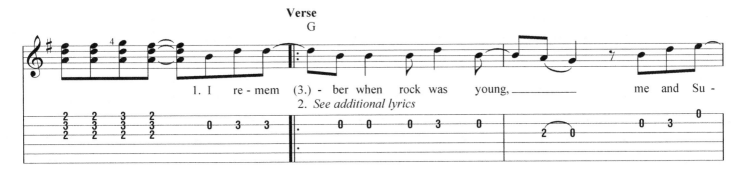

Verse

1. I re-mem (3.) - ber when rock was young, _____ me and Su-
2. *See additional lyrics*

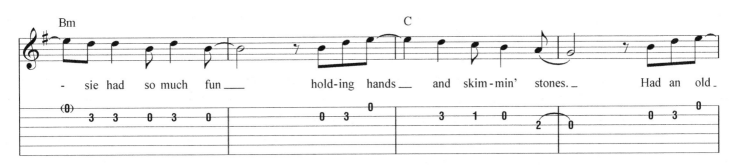

- sie had so much fun _____ hold-ing hands _____ and skim-min' stones. _____ Had an old _____

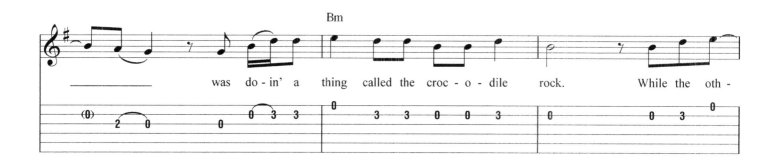

Chorus

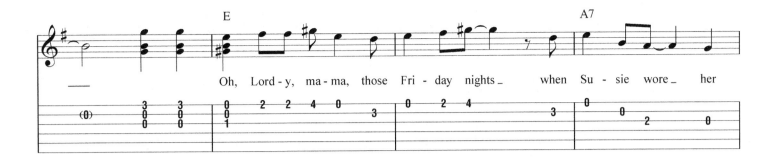

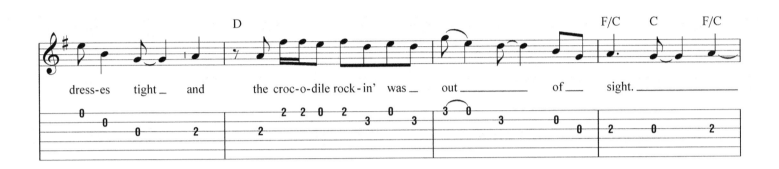

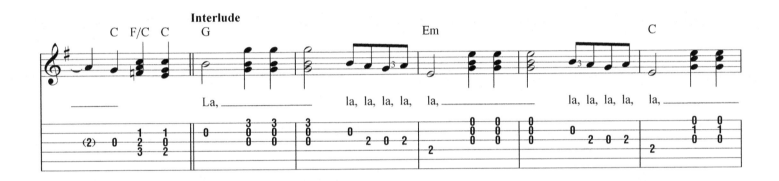

Additional Lyrics

2. But the years went by and rock just died.
   Susie went and left us for some foreign guy.
   Long nights cryin' by the record machine,
   Dreamin' of my Chevy and my old blue jeans.
   But they'll never kill the thrills we got
   Burnin' up to the crocodile rock.
   Learning fast as the weeks went past,
   We really thought the crocodile rock would last.

Beautiful Day

Words by Bono
Music by U2

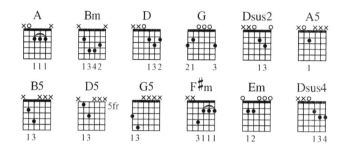

Strum Pattern: 1

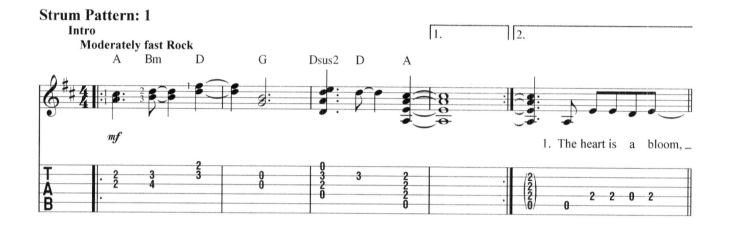

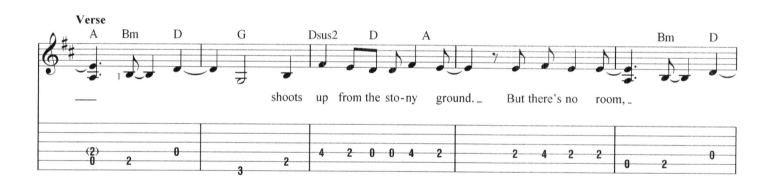

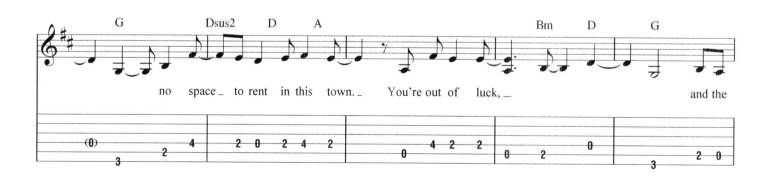

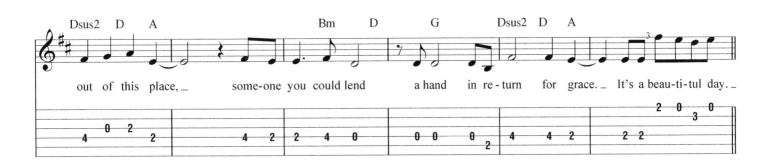

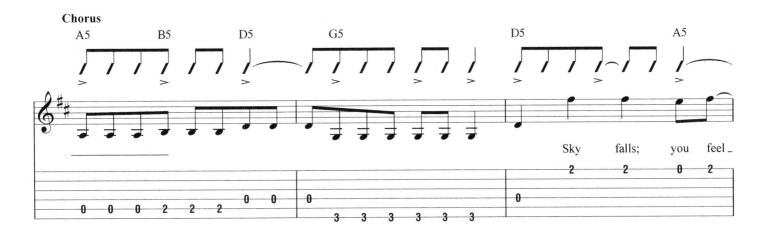

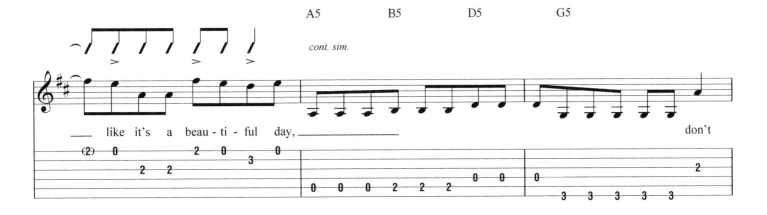

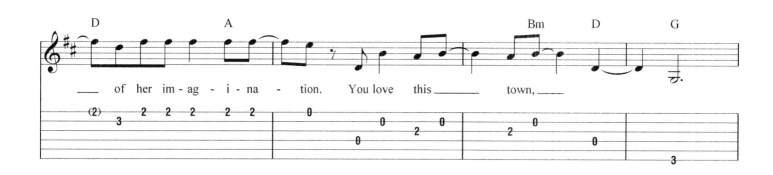

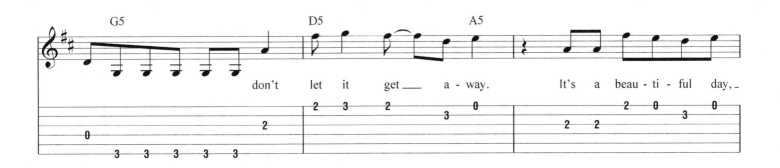

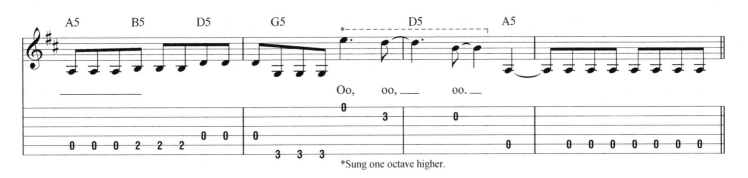

*Sung one octave higher.

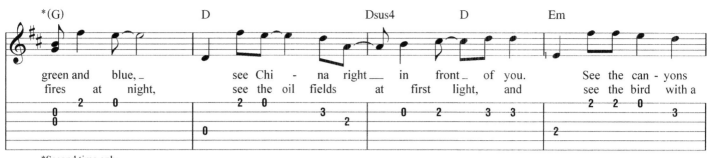

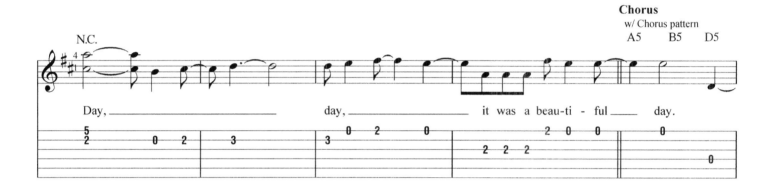

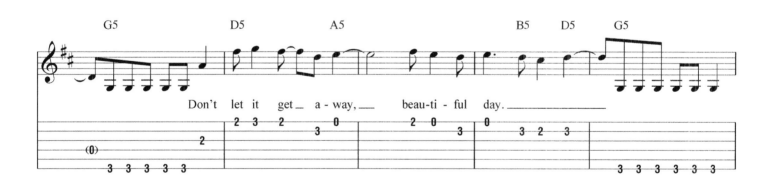

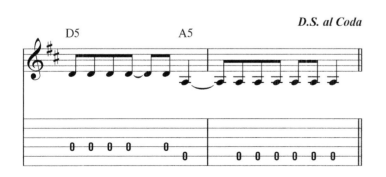

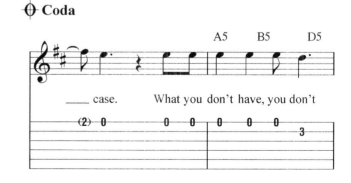

need it now.— What you don't know, you can feel __ it some - how. What you don't have, you don't

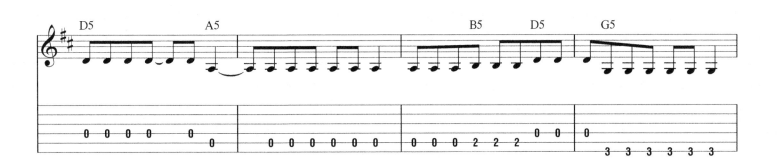

Outro-Chorus
w/ Chorus pattern

need it now,— don't need it now._____ Was a beau-ti-ful day._____

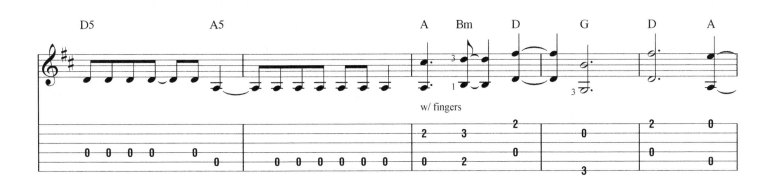

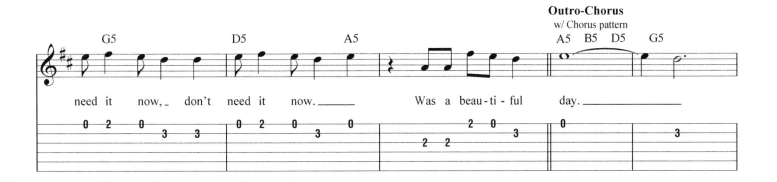

w/ fingers

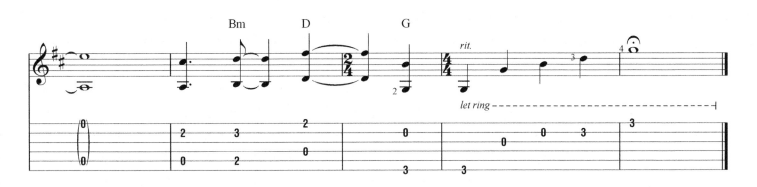

let ring -

Crazy Little Thing Called Love

Words and Music by Freddie Mercury

Strum Pattern: 1
Pick Pattern: 3

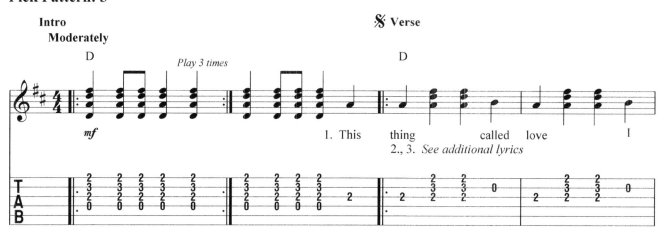

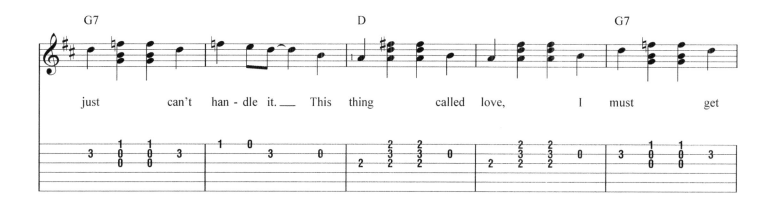

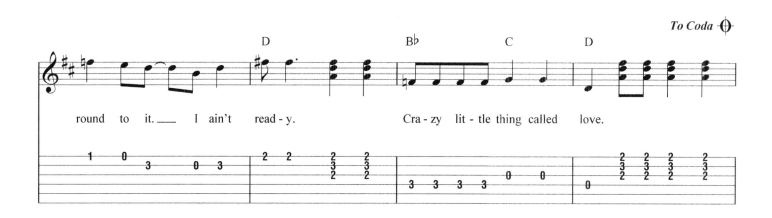

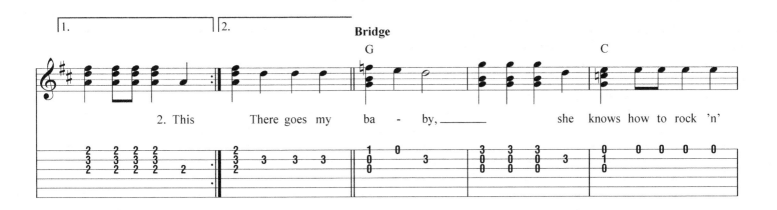

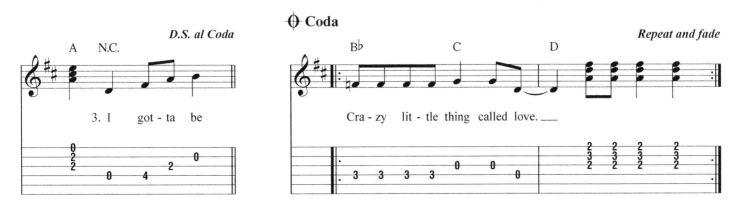

Additional Lyrics

2. This thing called love,
   It cries (like a baby) in a cradle all night.
   It swings, it jives,
   It shakes all over like a jellyfish.
   I kinda' like it.
   Crazy little thing called love.

3. I gotta be cool, relax,
   Get hip, get on my tracks.
   Take a backseat, hitchhike,
   And take a long ride on my motor bike
   Until I'm ready.
   Crazy little thing called love.

Don't Stop Believin'

Words and Music by Steve Perry, Neal Schon and Jonathan Cain

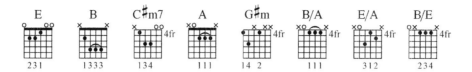

Strum Pattern: 3, 5
Pick Pattern: 3, 5

Intro
Moderate Rock

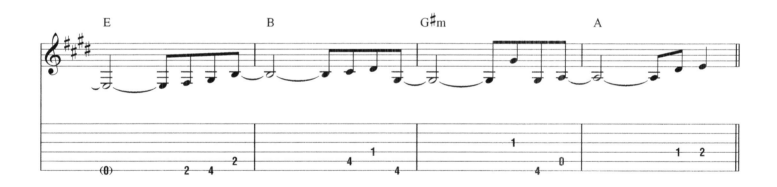

Verse

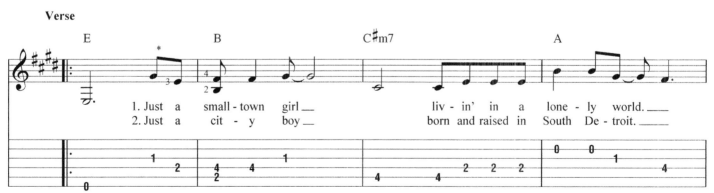

1. Just a small-town girl ___ liv-in' in a lone-ly world. ___
2. Just a cit-y boy ___ born and raised in South De-troit. ___

*Sung one octave higher throughout.

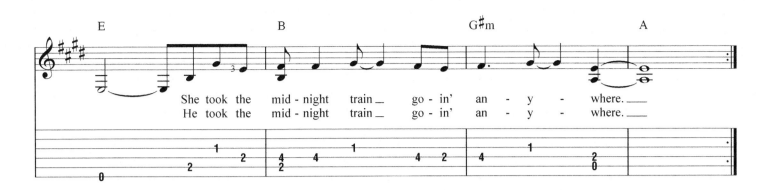

She took the mid-night train __ go-in' an-y - where. __
He took the mid-night train __ go-in' an-y - where. __

Interlude

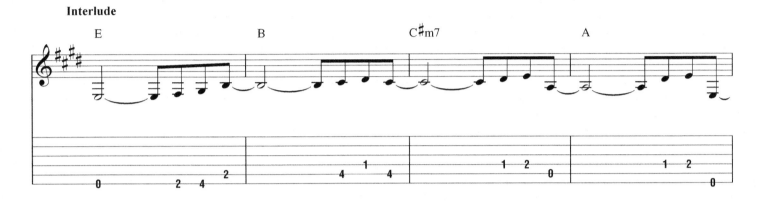

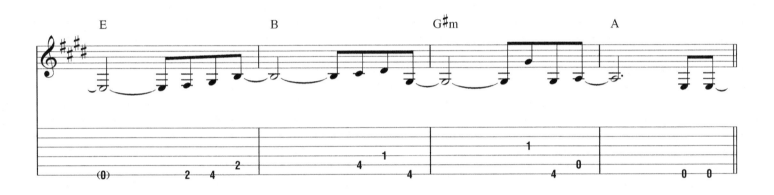

𝄋 Verse

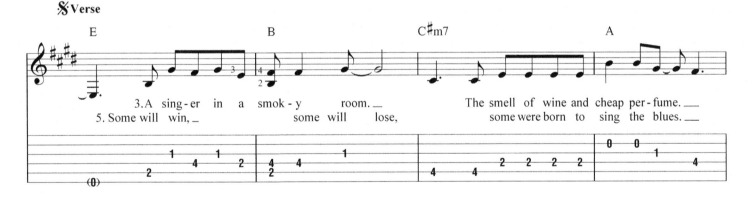

3. A sing-er in a smok-y room. __ The smell of wine and cheap per-fume. __
5. Some will win, __ some will lose, some were born to sing the blues. __

For a smile they can share the night. It goes on and on __ and on __ and on. __
Oh, the mov-ie nev - er ends; it goes on and on __ and on __ and on. __

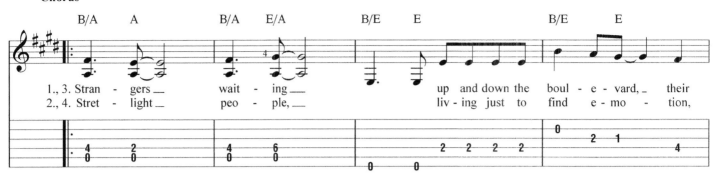

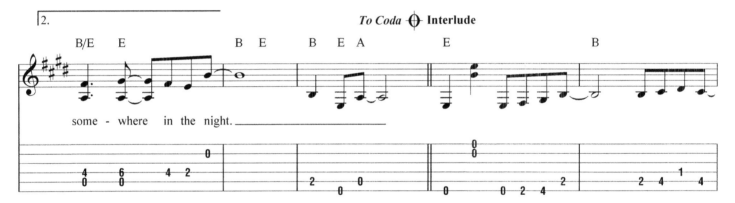

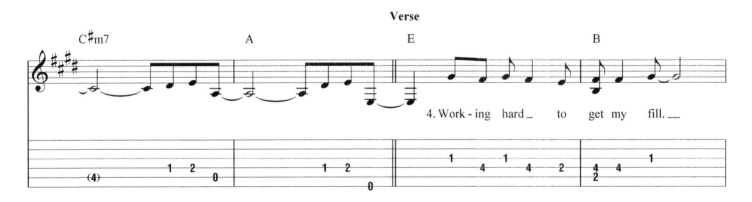

Verse

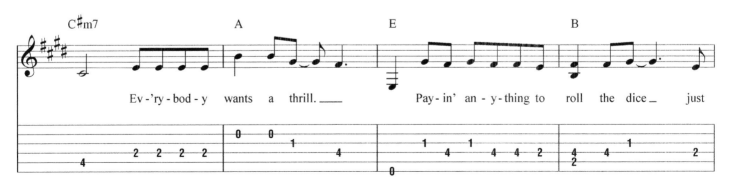

I Love Rock 'n Roll

Words and Music by Alan Merrill and Jake Hooker

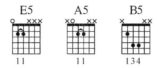

*Strum Pattern: 1, 5

Intro
Moderately slow rock, in 2

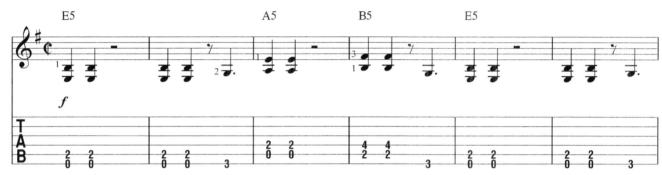

*Use pattern 10 for 2/4 meas.

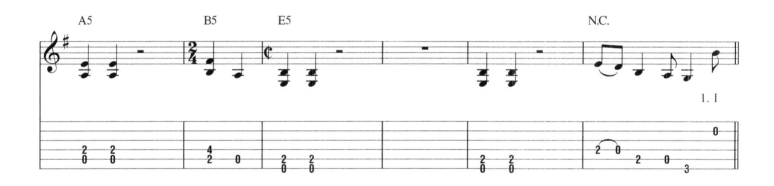

Verse

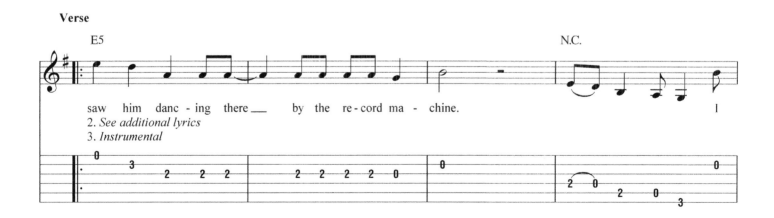

saw him danc-ing there ___ by the re-cord ma-chine.
2. See additional lyrics
3. Instrumental

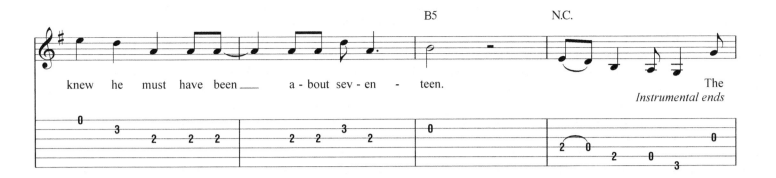

knew he must have been ___ a - bout sev - en - teen. The
Instrumental ends

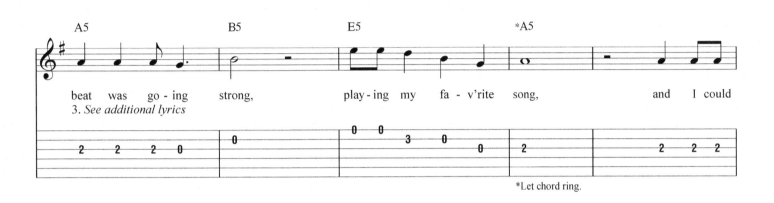

beat was go - ing strong, play - ing my fa - v'rite song, and I could
3. *See additional lyrics*

*Let chord ring.

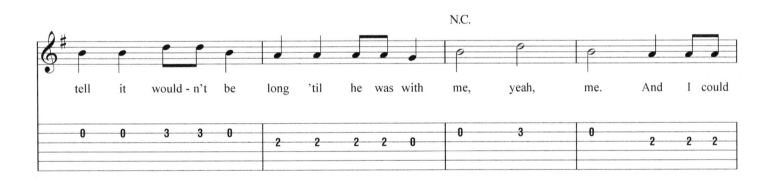

tell it would - n't be long 'til he was with me, yeah, me. And I could

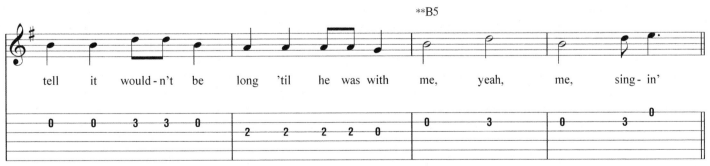

tell it would - n't be long 'til he was with me, yeah, me, sing - in'

**Third time, chords tacet.

w/ Intro pattern

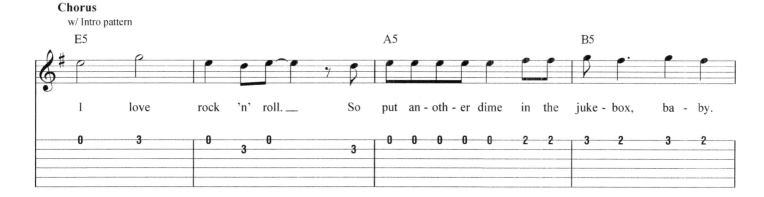

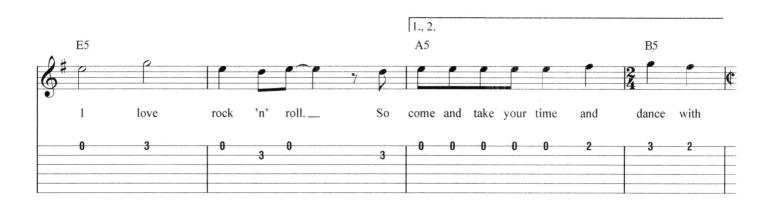

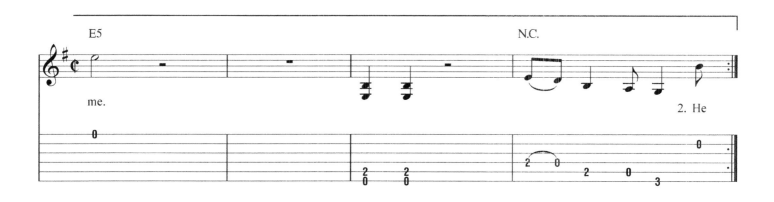

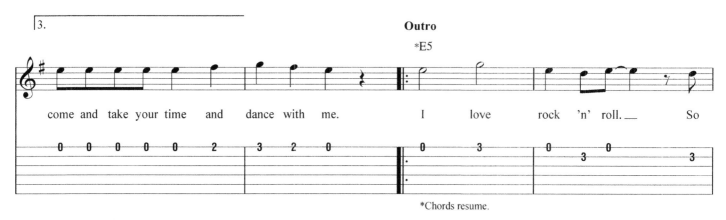

*Chords resume.

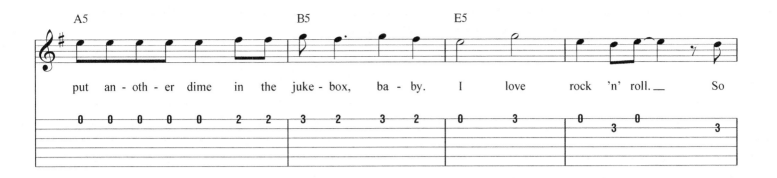

put an-oth-er dime in the juke-box, ba-by. I love rock 'n' roll. ___ So

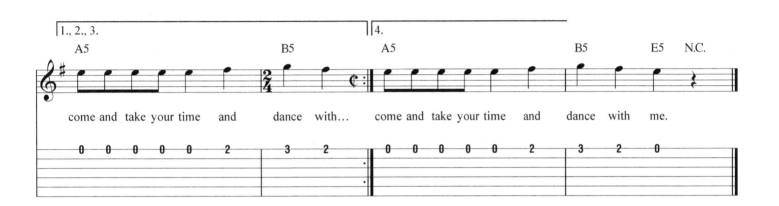

1., 2., 3.

come and take your time and dance with...

4.

come and take your time and dance with me.

Additional Lyrics

2. He smiled, so I got up and asked for his name.
   "That don't matter," he said,"'cause it's all the same."
   I said, "Can I take you home
   Where we can be alone?"
   And next we were moving on
   And he was with me, yeah, me.
   And next we were moving on.
   And he was with me, yeah, me, singin'…

3. *Instrumental*
   I said, "Can I take you home
   Where we can be alone?"
   And next we were moving on
   And he was with me, yeah, me.
   And we'll be movin' on and singin' that same old song,
   Yeah with me, singin'…

I'm a Believer

Words and Music by Neil Diamond

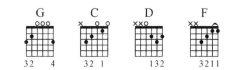

Strum Pattern: 3
Pick Pattern: 3

Intro
Bright Rock

*Optional: To match recording, place capo at 1st fret.

Verse

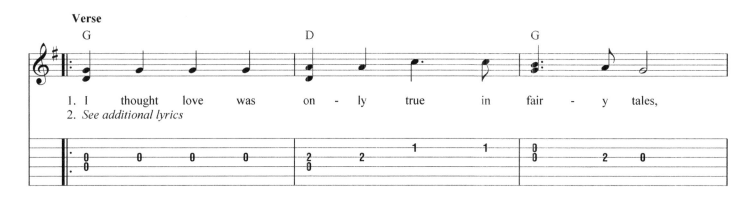

1. I thought love was on - ly true in fair - y tales,
2. *See additional lyrics*

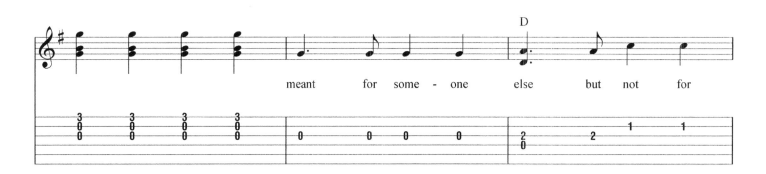

meant for some - one else but not for

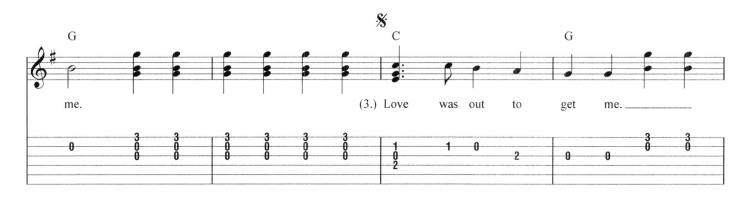

me.   (3.) Love was out to get me. _____

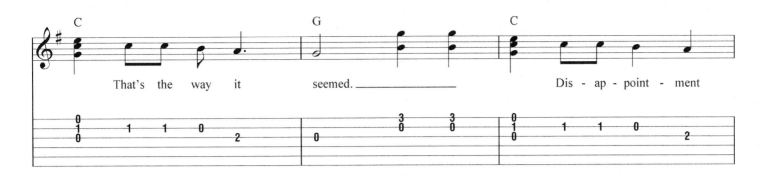

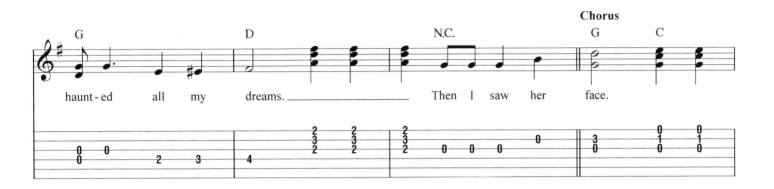

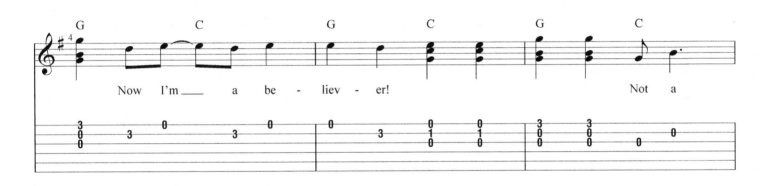

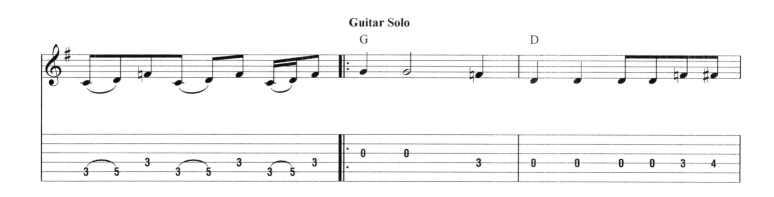

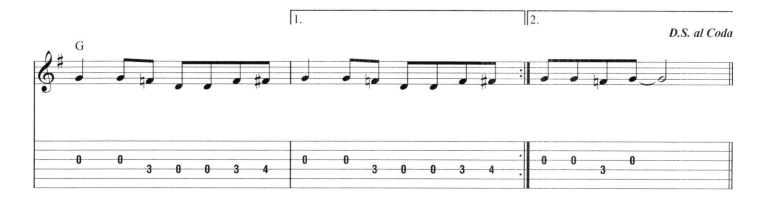

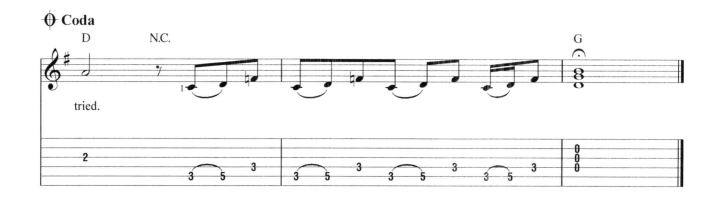

Additional Lyrics

2. I thought love was more or less a givin' thing.
   Seems the more I gave, the less I got.
   What's the use in tryin'?
   All you get is pain.
   When I needed sunshine, I got rain.

Rock and Roll All Nite

Words and Music by Paul Stanley and Gene Simmons

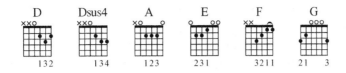

Strum Pattern: 2
Pick Pattern: 4

Intro   Verse
Moderately fast

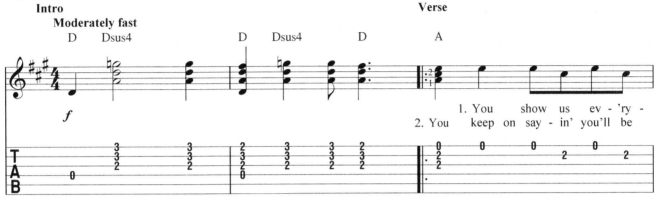

1. You show us ev - 'ry -
2. You keep on say - in' you'll be

thing you've got.   You keep on danc - in' and the room gets hot.
mine for a while.   You're look - in' fan - cy and I like your style.

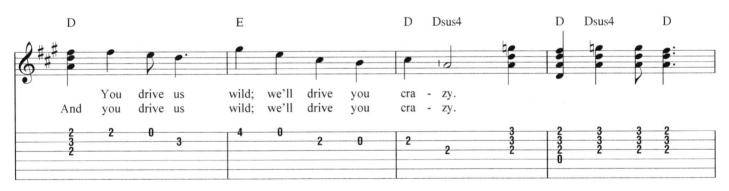

You drive us wild; we'll drive you cra - zy.
And you drive us wild; we'll drive you cra - zy.

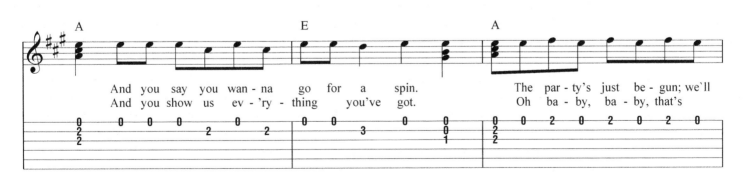

And you say you wan - na go for a spin.   The par - ty's just be - gun; we'll
And you show us ev - 'ry - thing you've got.   Oh ba - by, ba - by, that's

let you in.   You drive us wild; we'll drive you cra - zy.
quite a lot.   And you drive us wild; we'll drive you cra - zy.

Pre-Chorus

You keep on shout - in',   you keep on shout - in'.

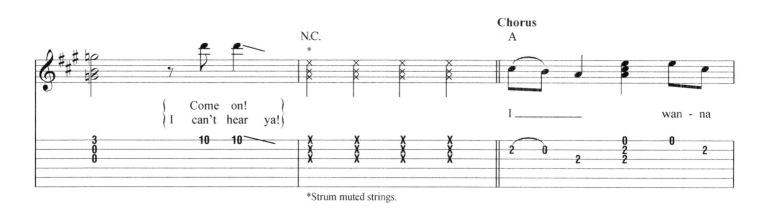

Chorus

N.C.
*

{ Come on! }
{ I can't hear ya! }

I _____ wan - na

*Strum muted strings.

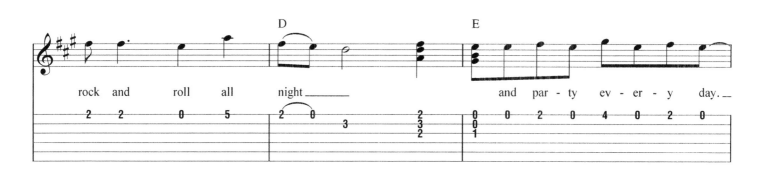

rock and roll all night _____   and par - ty ev - er - y day. __

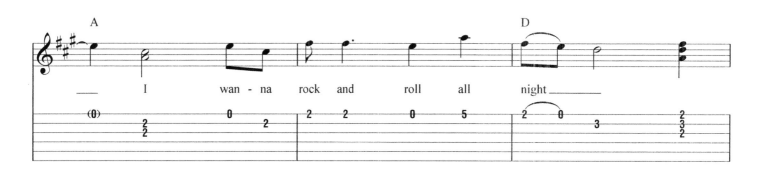

____ I wan - na rock and roll all night _____

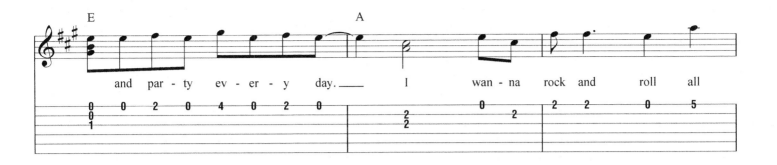

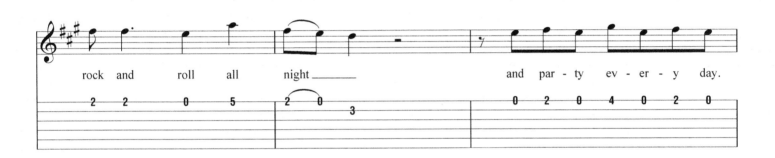

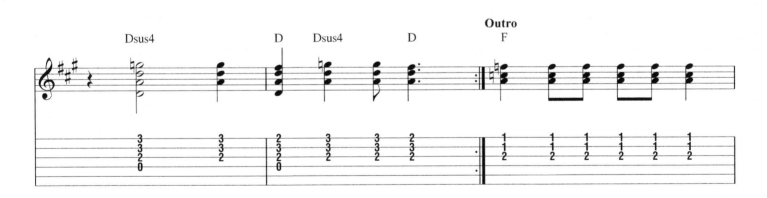

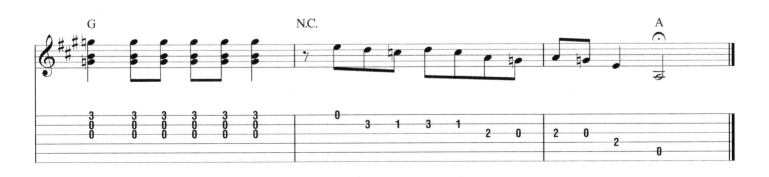

Let There Be Rock

Words and Music by Angus Young, Malcolm Young and Bon Scott

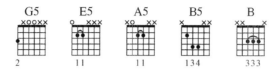

Strum Pattern: 1

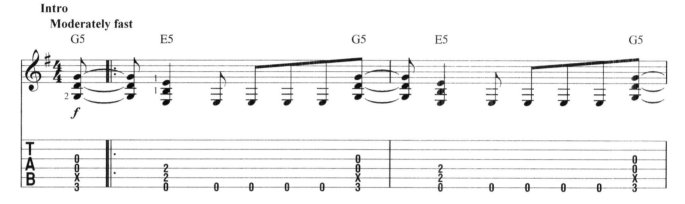

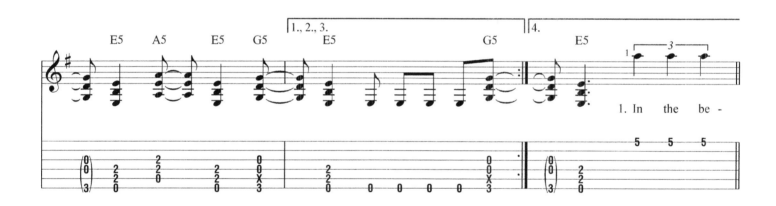

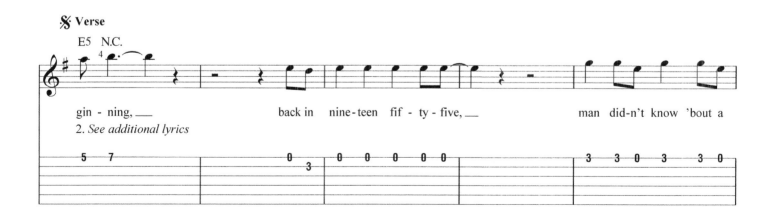

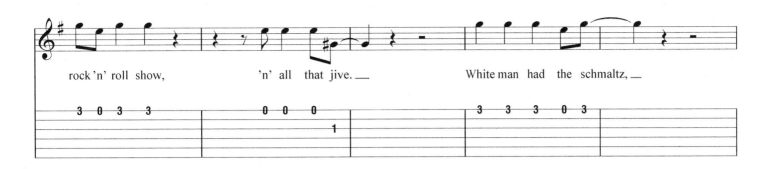

rock 'n' roll show,   'n' all that jive. __   White man had the schmaltz, __

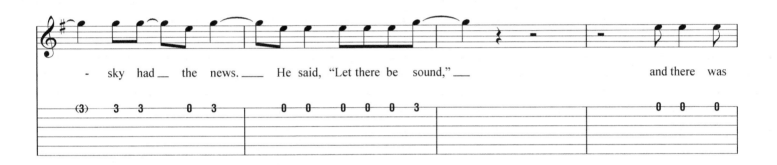

black man had the blues, _   no one knew what they was gon - na do, __ but Tchai - kov-

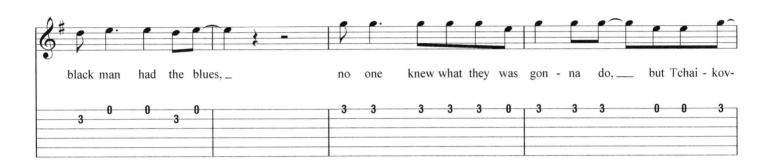

- sky had __ the news. __ He said, "Let there be sound," __   and there was

sound.   "Let there be light," __   and there was

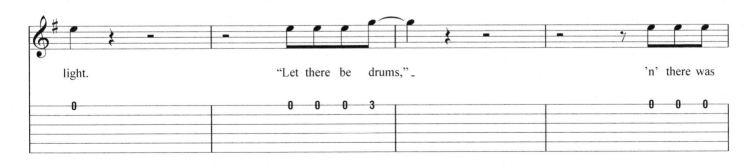

light.   "Let there be drums," _   'n' there was

drums.   "Let there be gui - tar."   There was gui - tar.

To Coda ⊕

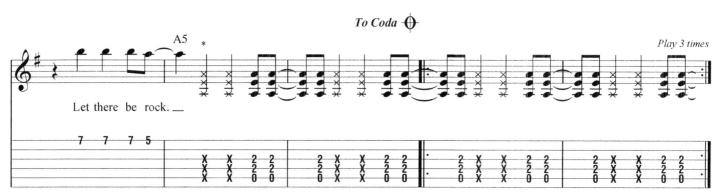

Let there be rock. __

*Strum muted strings.

Guitar Solo

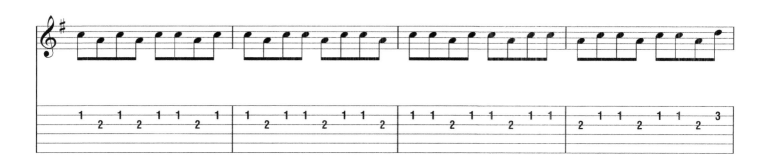

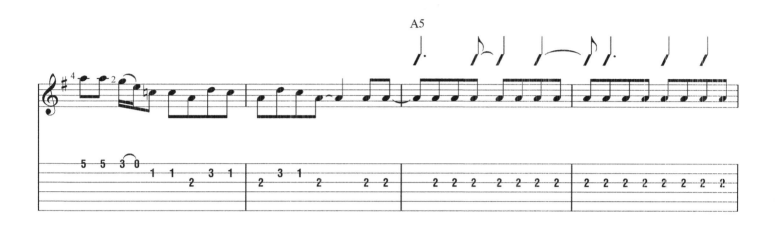

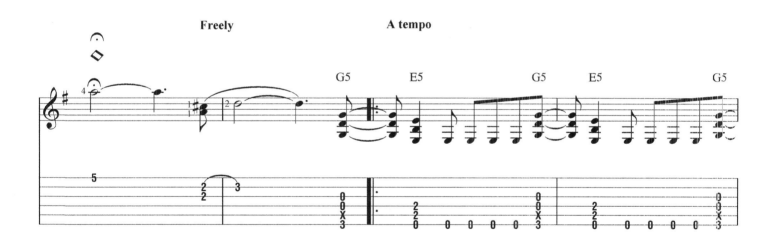

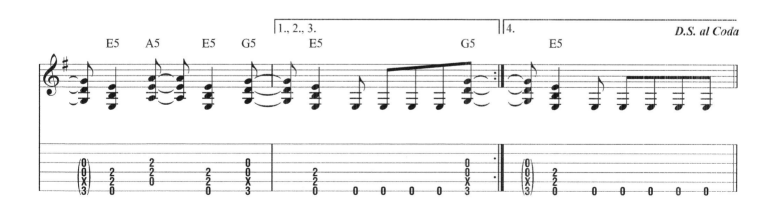

Coda

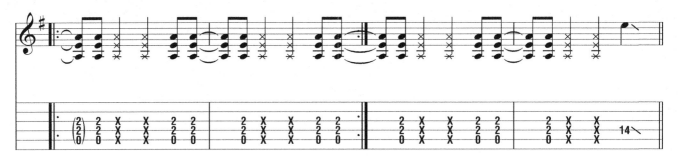

Interlude

A5

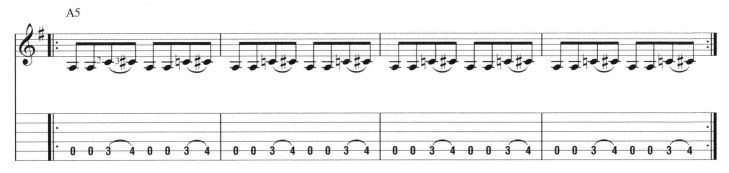

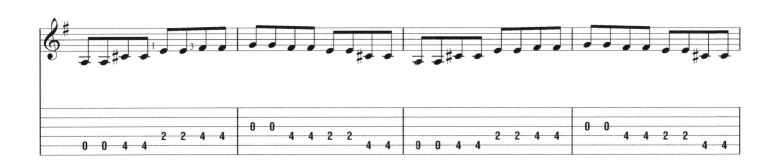

B5

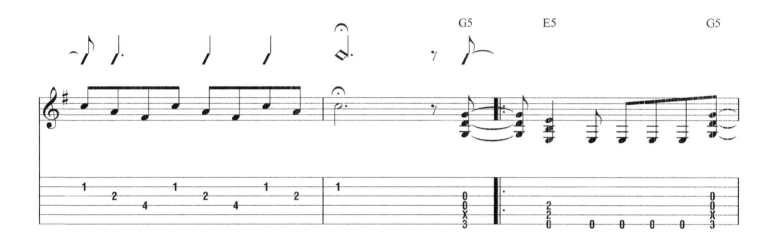

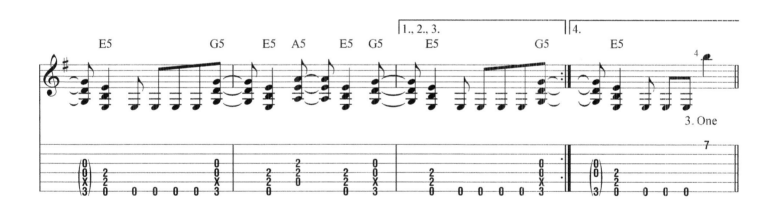

3. One

Verse

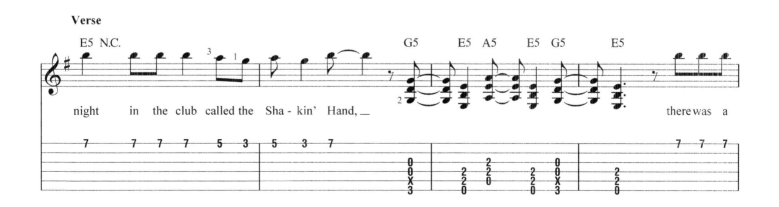

night in the club called the Sha - kin' Hand, ___ there was a

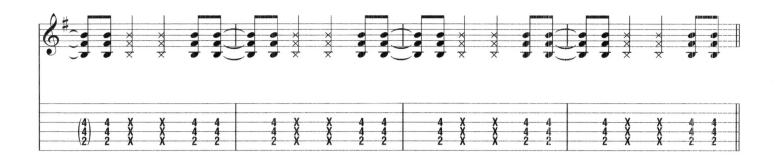

Play 8 times

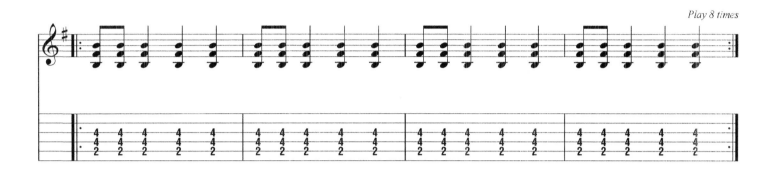

Free time

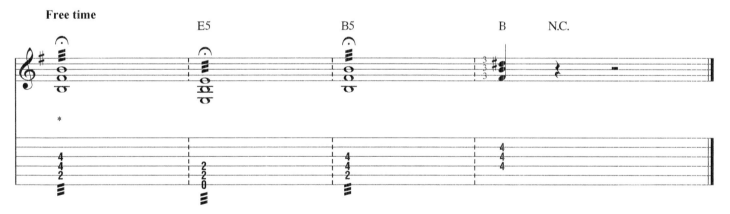

*Tremolo picking: The notes are picked
as rapidly and continuously as possible.

Additional Lyrics

2. And it came to pass
That rock 'n' roll was born.
And all across the land, ev'ry rockin' band
Was blowin' up a storm.
And the guitar man got famous.
And the business man got rich.
And in ev'ry bar there was a superstar
With a seven year itch.
There were fifty million fingers
Learnin' how to play,
And you could hear the fingers pickin'.
And this is what they had to say,
"Let there be light, sound, drums, guitar,
Ow! Let there be rock."

Lookin' Out My Back Door

Words and Music by John Fogerty

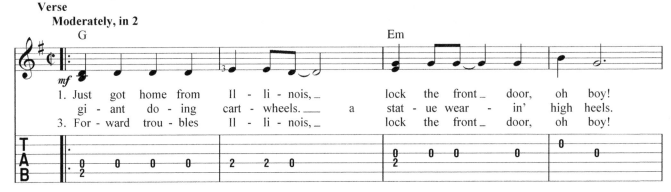

Strum Pattern: 3, 4
Pick Pattern: 3, 4

Verse
Moderately, in 2

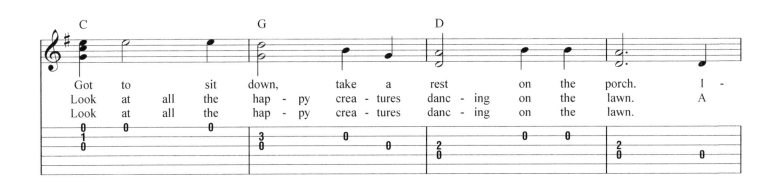

1. Just got home from Il - li - nois, __ lock the front __ door, oh boy!
   gi - ant do - ing cart - wheels. __ a stat - ue wear - in' high heels.
3. For - ward trou - bles Il - li - nois, __ lock the front __ door, oh boy!

Got to sit down, take a rest on the porch. I -
Look at all the hap - py crea - tures danc - ing on the lawn. A
Look at all the hap - py crea - tures danc - ing on the lawn.

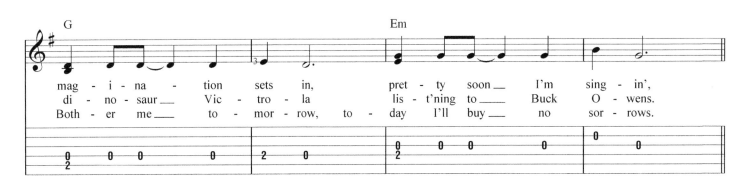

mag - i - na - tion sets in, pret - ty soon __ I'm sing - in',
di - no - saur __ Vic - tro - la lis - t'ning to __ Buck O - wens.
Both - er me __ to - mor - row, to - day I'll buy __ no sor - rows.

Chorus

To Coda ⊕   1.

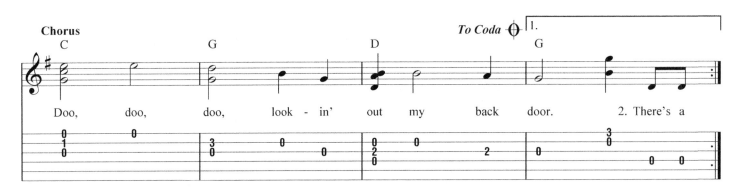

Doo, doo, doo, look - in' out my back door.   2. There's a

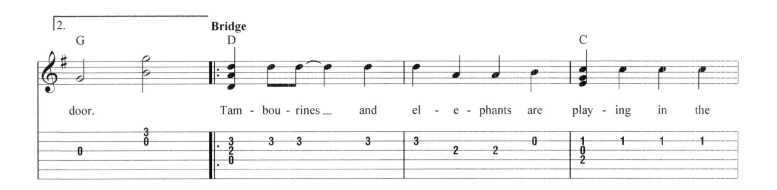

door.　Tam - bou - rines and el - e - phants are play - ing in the

band.　Won't you take a ride on the fly - in'

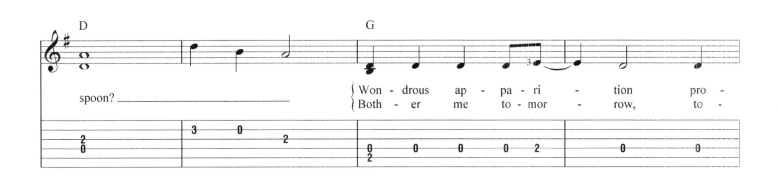

spoon?　{ Won - drous ap - pa - ri - tion pro -
{ Both - er me to - mor - row, to -

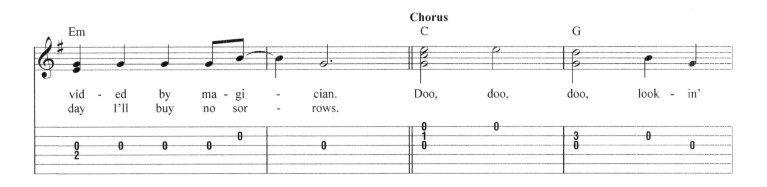

vid - ed by ma - gi - cian.　Doo, doo, doo, look - in'
day I'll buy no sor - rows.

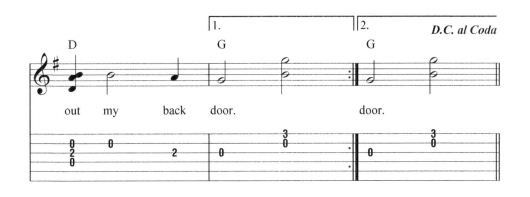

out my back door.　　door.

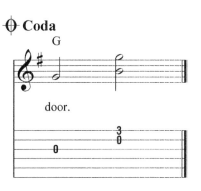

door.

Three Little Birds

Words and Music by Bob Marley

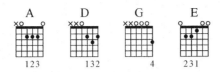

Strum Pattern: 2

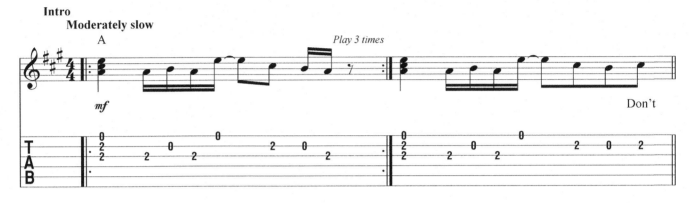

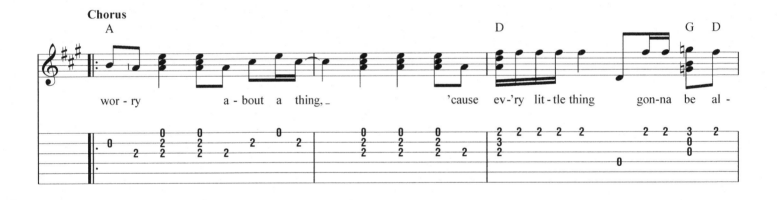

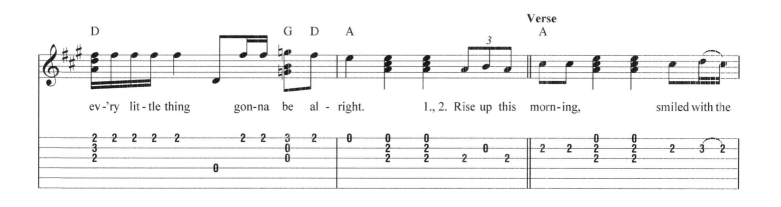

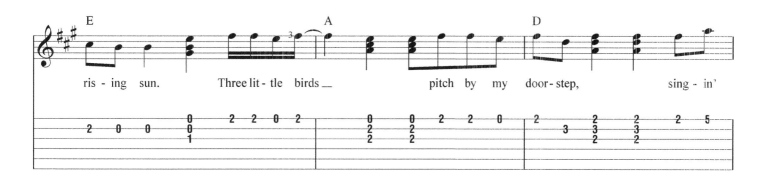

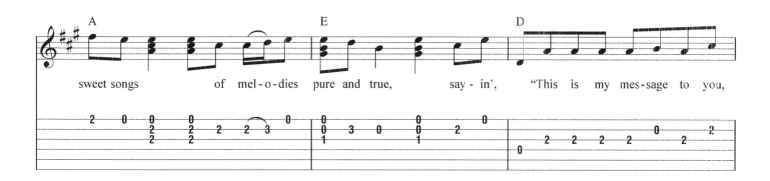

Walking on Sunshine

Words and Music by Kimberley Rew

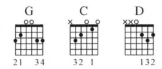

*Capo III

Strum Pattern: 6, 4
Pick Pattern: 1, 6

Verse
Moderately, in 2

1. I used to think may - be you loved ___ me; now, ba - by, I'm ___ sure.
used to think may - be you loved ___ me; now I know that it's true.

*Optional: To match recording, place capo at 3rd fret.

And I just can't wait ___ till the day ___
And I don't wan - na spend ___ my whole life ___

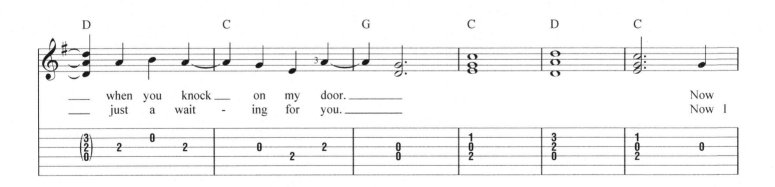

___ when you knock ___ on my door. ___
___ just a wait - ing for you. ___

Now
Now I

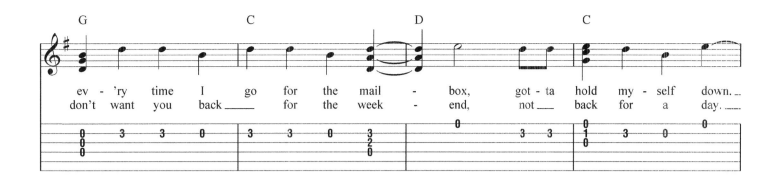

ev - 'ry time I go for the mail - box, got - ta hold my - self down.
don't want you back ___ for the week - end, not ___ back for a day. ___

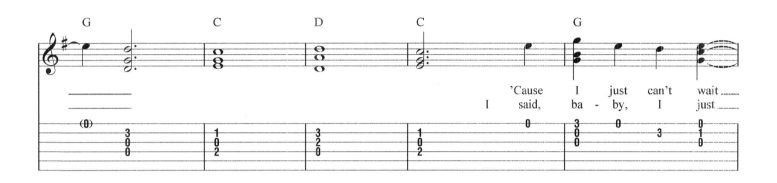

___ ___ 'Cause I just can't wait ___
___ ___ I said, ba - by, I just ___

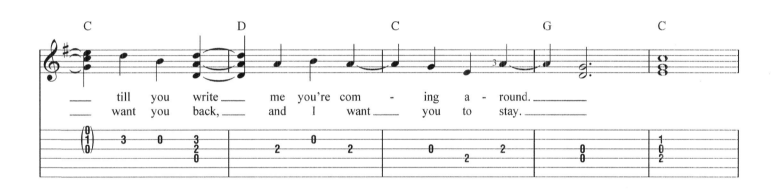

___ till you write ___ me you're com - ing a - round. ___
___ want you back, ___ and I want ___ you to stay. ___

%. **Chorus**

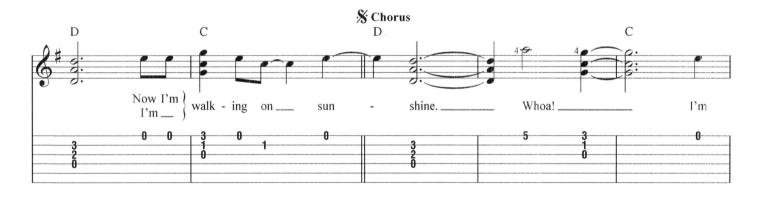

Now I'm
I'm ___ } walk - ing on ___ sun - shine. ___ Whoa! ___ I'm

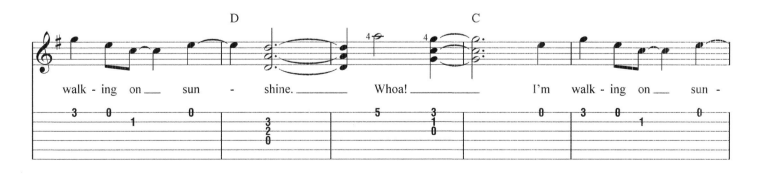

walk - ing on ___ sun - shine. ___ Whoa! ___ I'm walk - ing on ___ sun -

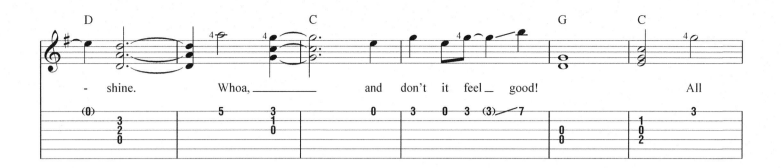

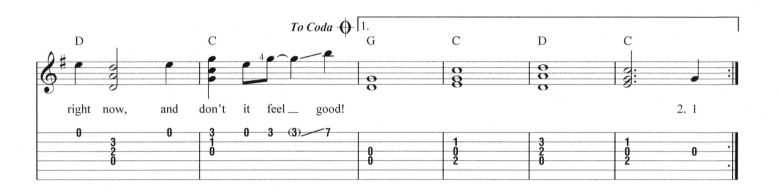

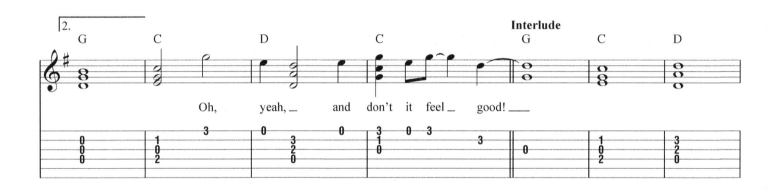

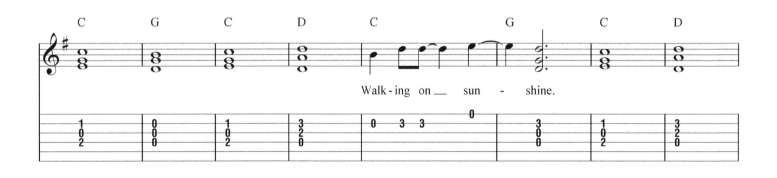

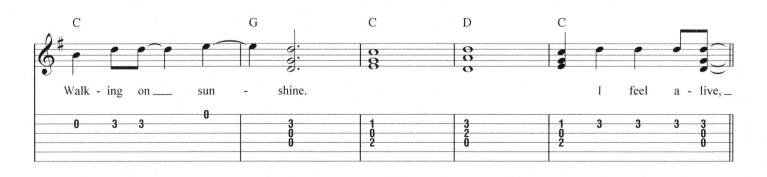

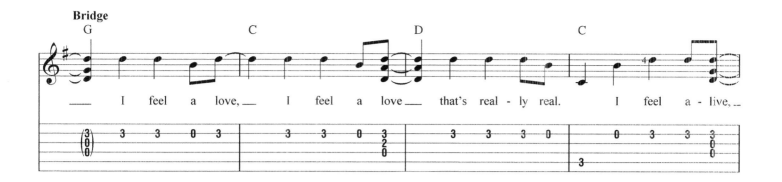

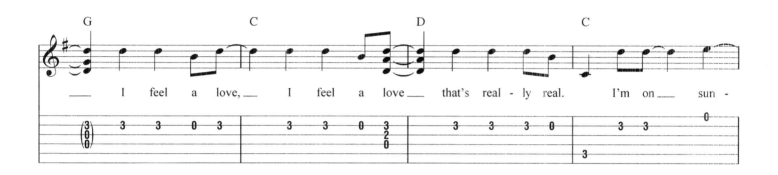

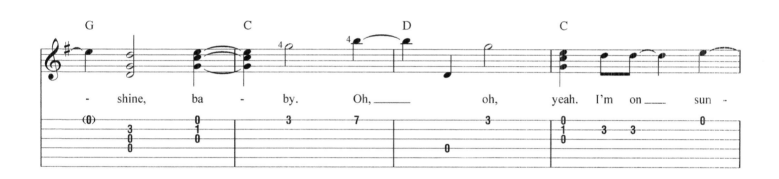

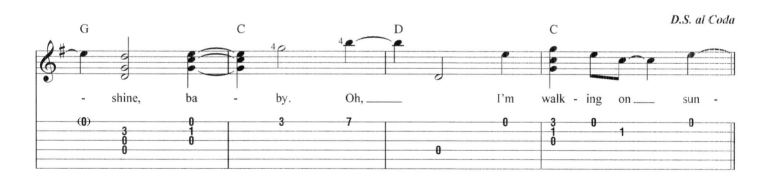

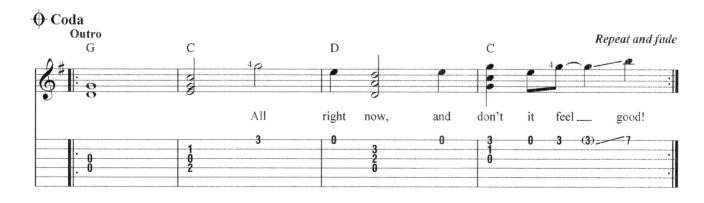

We Got the Beat

Words and Music by Charlotte Caffey

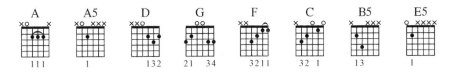

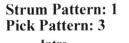

Strum Pattern: 1
Pick Pattern: 3

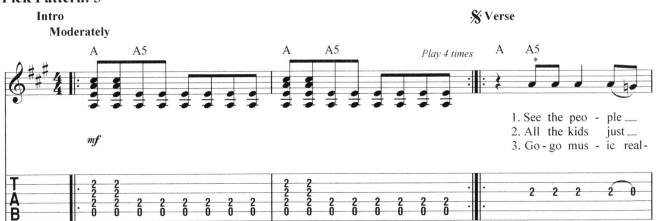

1. See the peo - ple __
2. All the kids just __
3. Go - go mus - ic real-

*Sung one octave higher.

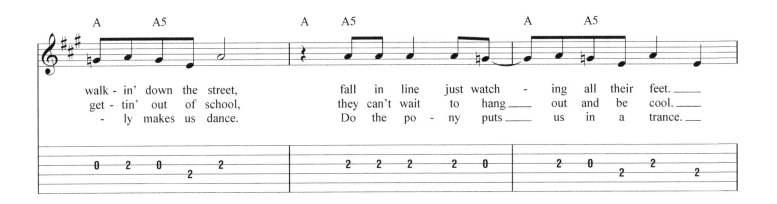

walk - in' down the street,   fall in line just watch - ing all their feet. __
get - tin' out of school,   they can't wait to hang __ out and be cool. __
- ly makes us dance.   Do the po - ny puts __ us in a trance. __

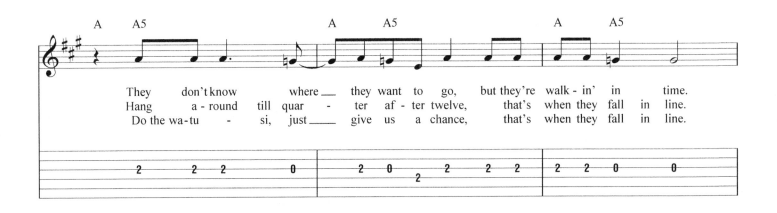

They don't know where __ they want to go, but they're walk - in' in time.
Hang a - round till quar - ter af - ter twelve, that's when they fall in line.
Do the wa - tu - si, just __ give us a chance, that's when they fall in line.

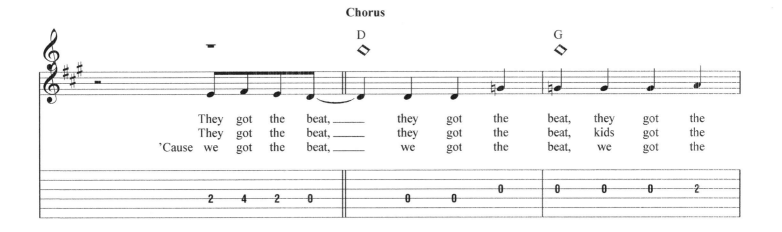

Chorus

They got the beat,_____ they got the beat, they got the
They got the beat,_____ they got the beat, kids got the
'Cause we got the beat,_____ we got the beat, we got the

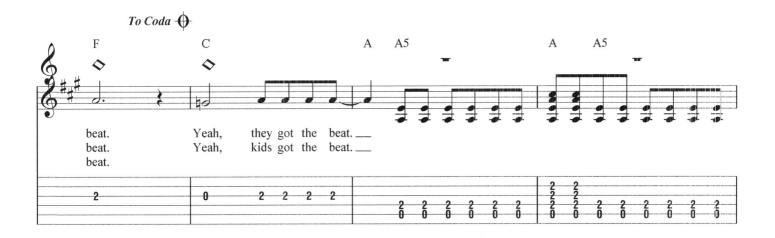

To Coda

beat. Yeah, they got the beat. ___
beat. Yeah, kids got the beat. ___
beat.

Instrumental

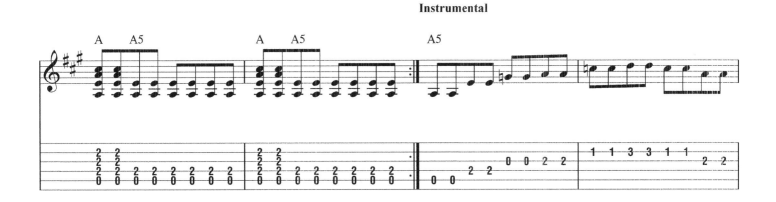

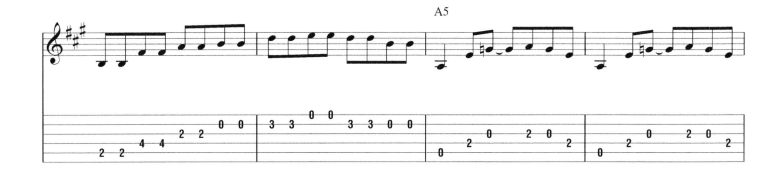

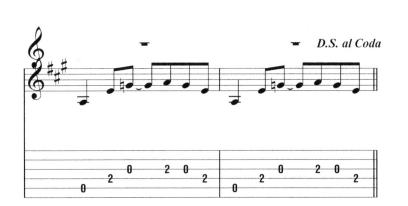

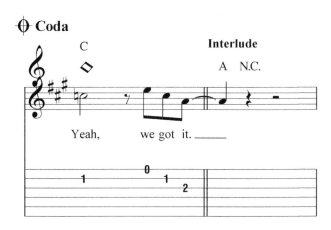

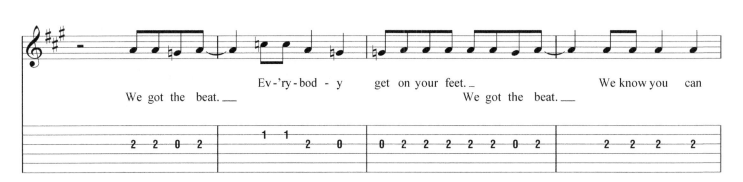

dance to the beat. _____ Jump back, ___ get down. ___ Round and round and
We got the beat. _____ We got the beat. ___

Outro

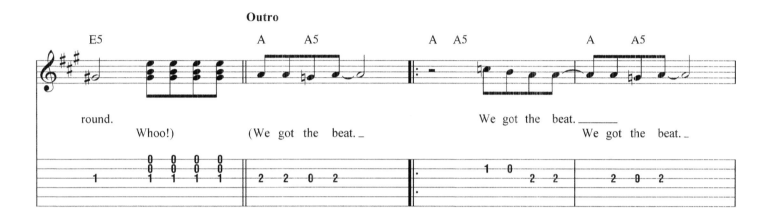

round.
Whoo!) (We got the beat. _ We got the beat. _____
We got the beat. _

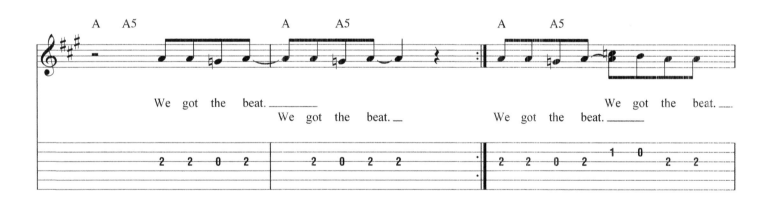

We got the beat. _____ We got the beat. _____
We got the beat. _ We got the beat. _____

_____ We got the beat. _____
We got the beat. _ We got the beat.) _____

We Will Rock You

Words and Music by Brian May

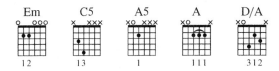

Strum Pattern: 1
Pick Pattern: 1

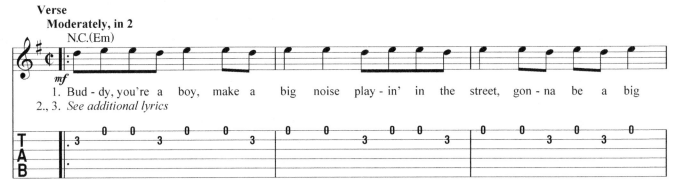

1. Bud-dy, you're a boy, make a big noise play-in' in the street, gon-na be a big
2., 3. *See additional lyrics*

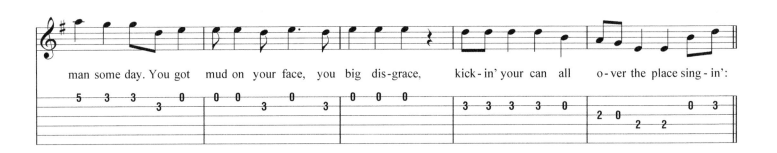

man some day. You got mud on your face, you big dis-grace, kick-in' your can all o-ver the place sing-in':

Chorus

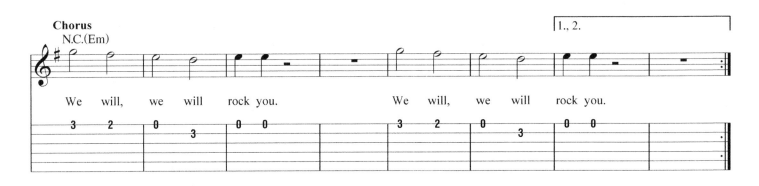

We will, we will rock you. We will, we will rock you.

rock you. We will, we will rock you. We will, we will

Guitar Solo

rock you.

*Let chord ring.

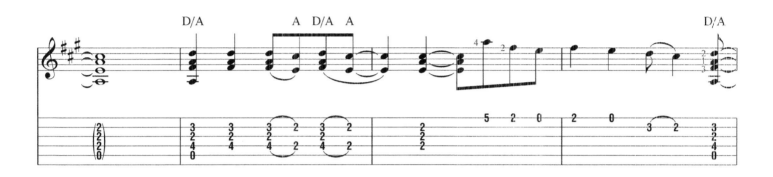

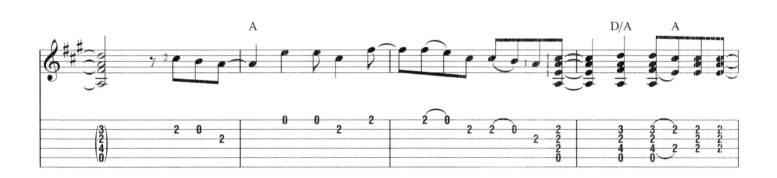

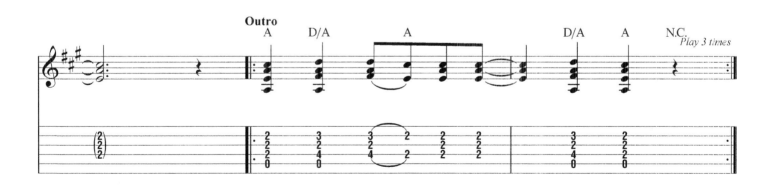

Outro

Play 3 times

Additional Lyrics

2. Buddy, you're a young man, hard man shoutin' in the street,
    Gonna take on the world some day.
    You got blood on your face,
    You big disgrace,
    Wavin' your banner all over the place.

3. Buddy, you're an old man, poor man pleadin' with your eyes.
    Gonna make you some peace someday.
    You got mud on your face,
    You big disgrace,
    Somebody better put you back into your place.

What I Like About You

Words and Music by Michael Skill, Wally Palamarchuk and James Marinos

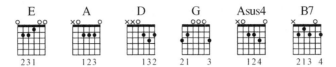

Strum Pattern: 3
Pick Pattern: 3

Intro
Moderately fast

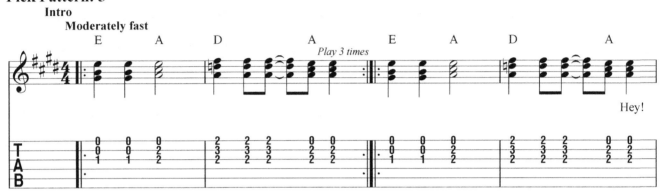

Hey!

Unh - huh

1. What I like a - bout

Verse

you,

3. *See additional lyrics*

you hold me tight. __

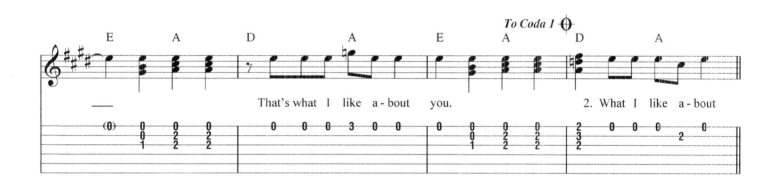

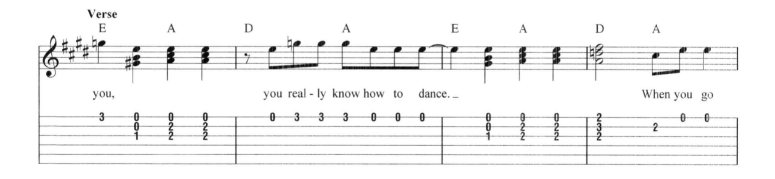

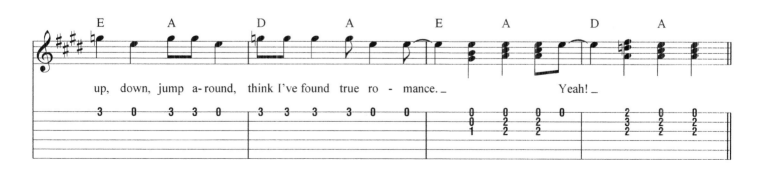

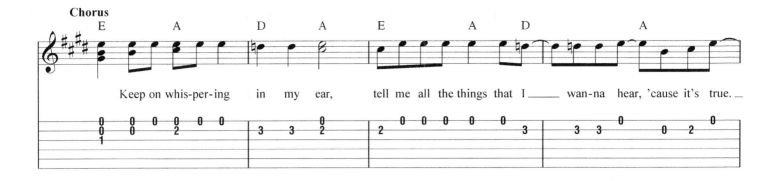

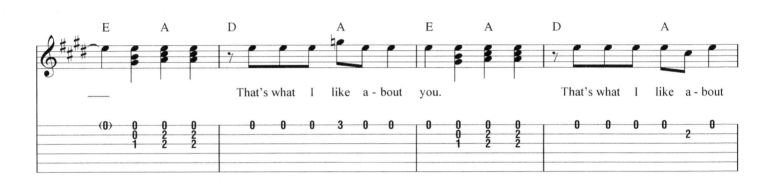

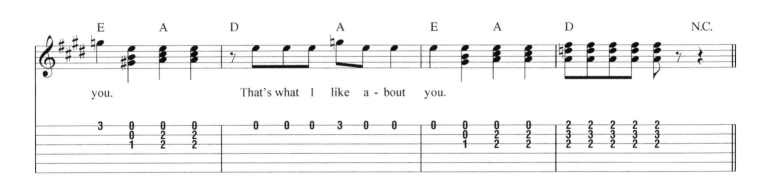

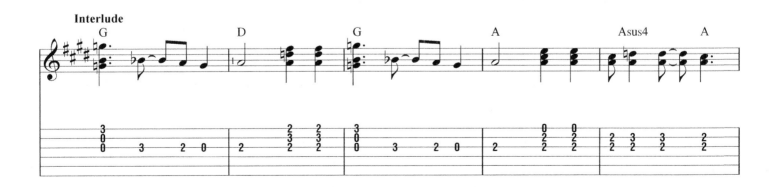

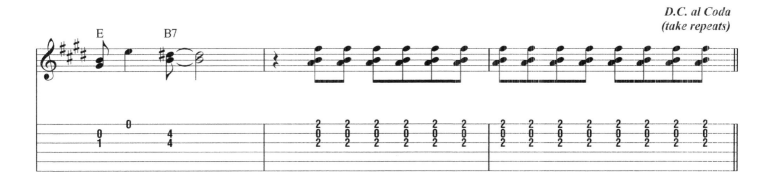

⊕ Coda

That's what I like a - bout you. *Whisper: That's what I like a - bout*

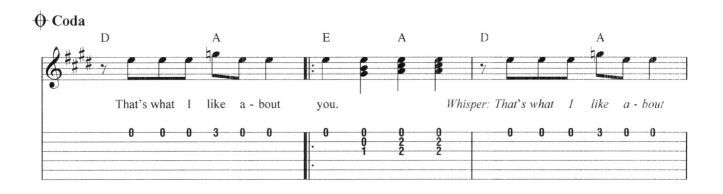

you. *That's what I like a - bout you.* Hey!

Outro *Repeat and fade*

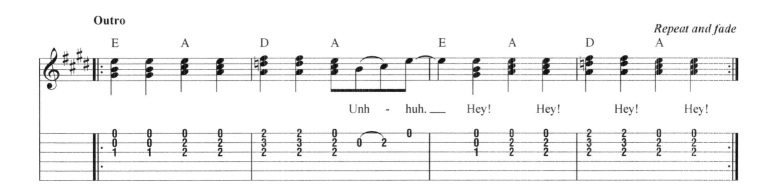

Unh - huh. ___ Hey! Hey! Hey! Hey!

Additional Lyrics

3. What I like about you,
   You keep me warm at night.
   Never wanna let go,
   Know you make me feel alright. Yeah!

Wild Thing

Words and Music by Chip Taylor

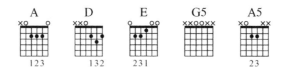

Strum Pattern: 3
Pick Pattern: 3

Chorus
Moderate Rock

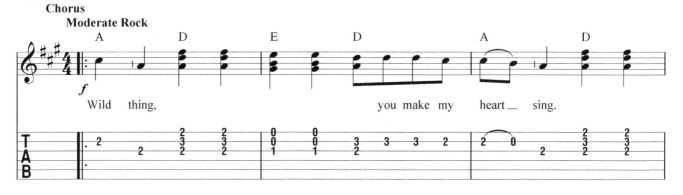

Wild thing, you make my heart __ sing.

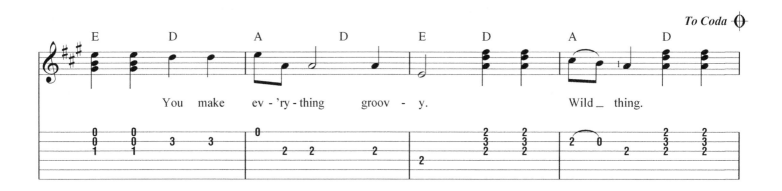

You make ev - 'ry - thing groov - y. Wild __ thing.

To Coda ⊕

Verse

Spoken: 1., 2. Wild thing I _____ think { I love you, / you move me, }

*Let chords ring throughout Verse.

Sung: but I wan-na know__ for sure.__   Spoken: Come on and

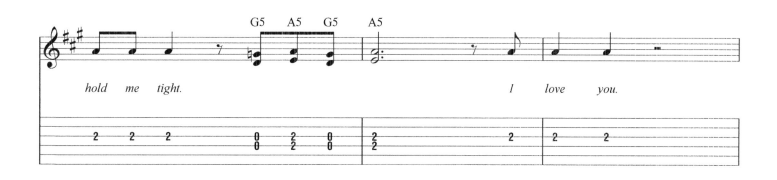

hold me tight.   I love you.

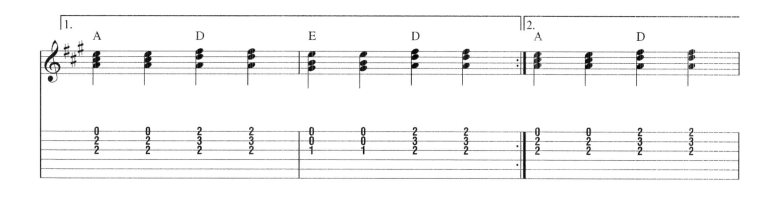

$\oplus$ **Coda**

D.C. al Coda   **Outro**   *Repeat and fade*

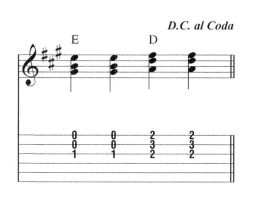

C'm'-on, c'm'-on, wild thing.

You're My Best Friend

Words and Music by John Deacon

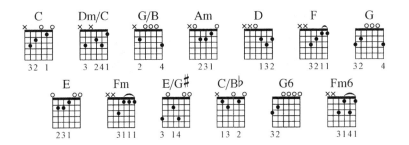

Strum Pattern: 3
Pick Pattern: 3

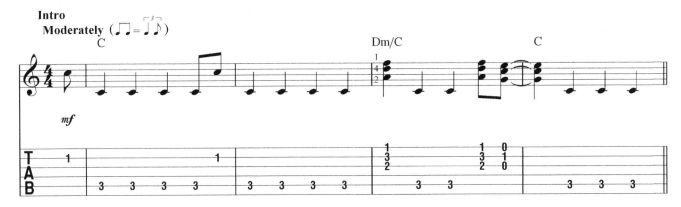

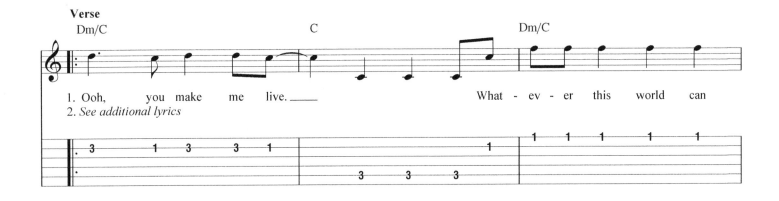

1. Ooh, you make me live.____ What-ev-er this world can
2. *See additional lyrics*

give to me.____ It's you, you're all I ____ see.____

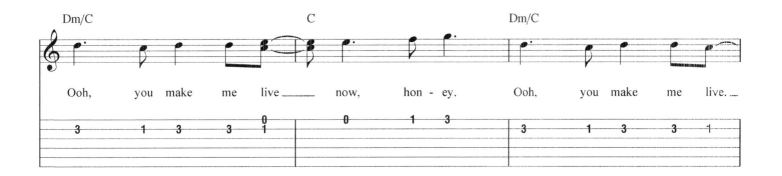

Ooh, you make me live _____ now, hon - ey. Ooh, you make me live. __

__ Oh, _____ you're the best _____ friend _____ that I _____

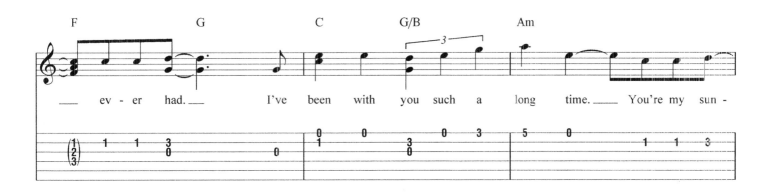

__ ev - er had. __ I've been with you such a long time. __ You're my sun -

- shine _____ and I want _____ you to know __ that my feel - ings are true. __ I

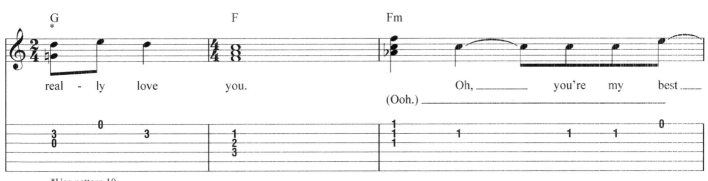

real - ly love you. Oh, _____ you're my best _____
(Ooh.) _____

*Use pattern 10.

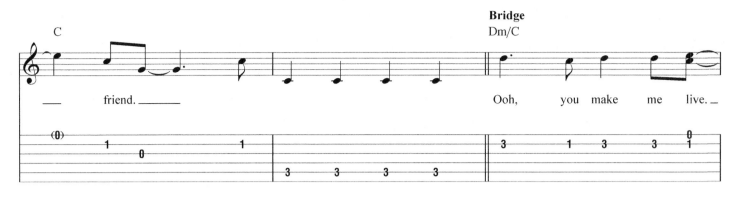

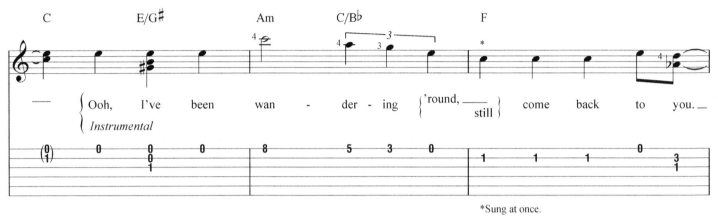

*Sung at once.

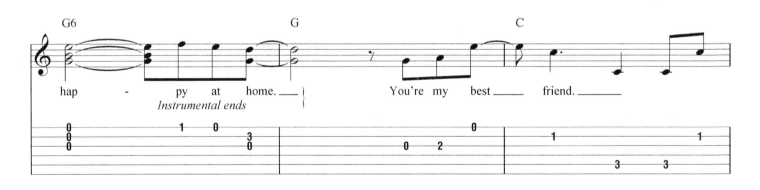

Outro

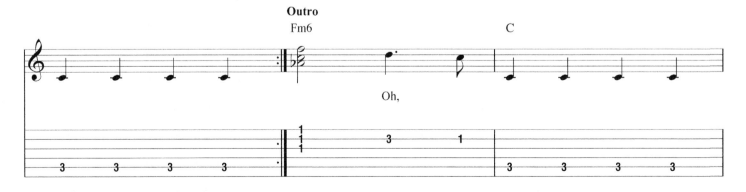

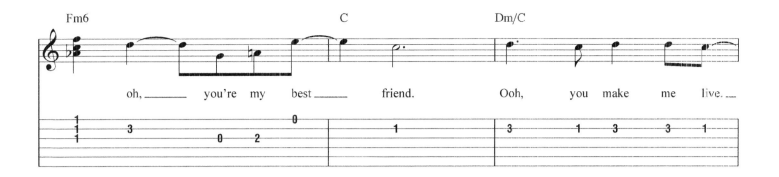

oh, _____ you're my best _____ friend. Ooh, you make me live. __

__ Ooh, you're my best friend. __

Additional Lyrics

2. Ooh, you make me live.
   Whenever this world is cruel to me.
   I got you to help me forgive.
   Ooh, you make me live now, honey.
   Ooh, you make me live.
   Oh, you're the first one when things turn out bad.
   You know I'll never be lonely, you're my only one.
   And I love the things, I really love the things that you do.
   Oh, you're my best friend.

Rock This Town

Words and Music by Brian Setzer

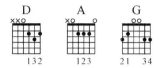

Strum Pattern: 6
Pick Pattern: 4

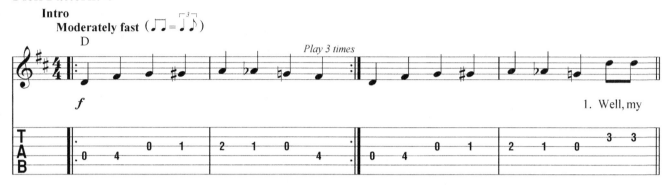

1. Well, my

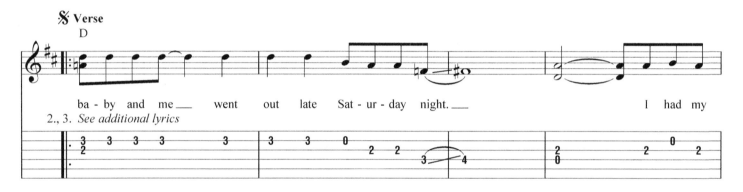

ba - by and me ___ went out late Sat - ur - day night. ___ I had my
2., 3. *See additional lyrics*

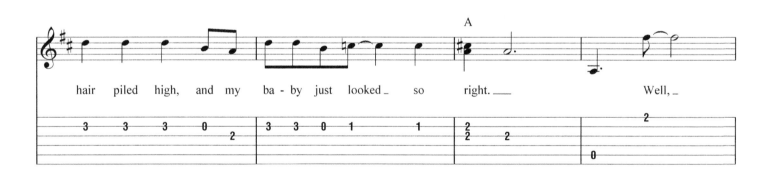

hair piled high, and my ba - by just looked _ so right. ___ Well, _

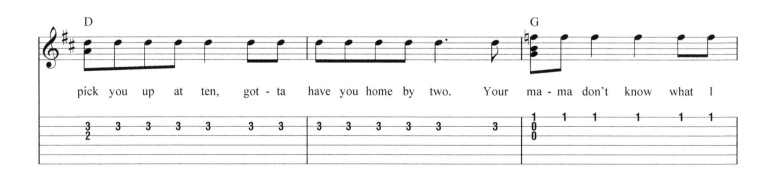

pick you up at ten, got - ta have you home by two. Your ma - ma don't know what I

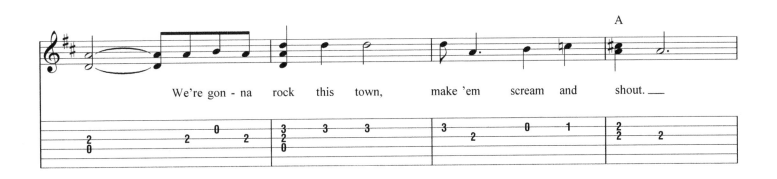

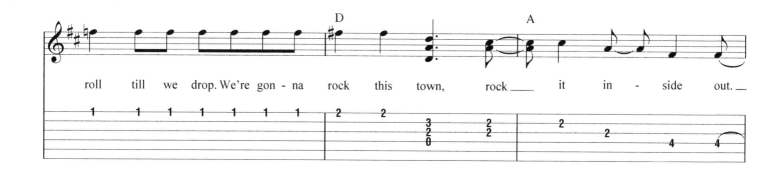

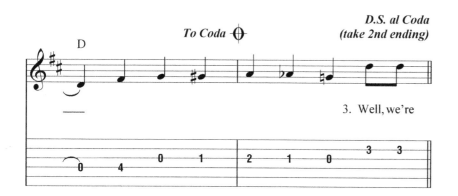

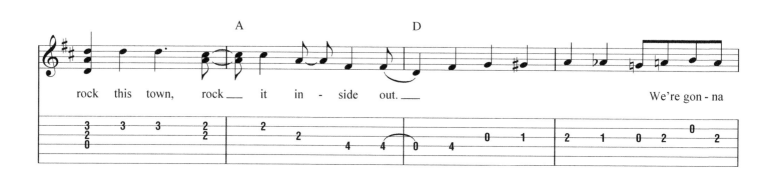

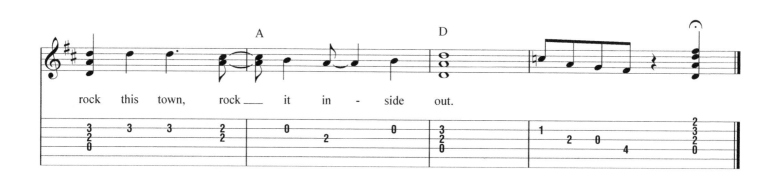

Additional Lyrics

2. Well, we found a little place that really didn't look half bad.
I had whiskey on the rocks and change of a dollar for the jukebox.
Well, I put a quarter right into that can,
But all it played was disco, man.
Come on, pretty baby, let's get out of here right away.

3. Well, we're havin' a ball just boppin' on the big dance floor.
Well, there's a real square cat; he looks a nineteen-seventy-four.
Well, you look at me once, you look at me twice.
Look at me again and there's gonna be a fight.
We're gonna rock this town, we're gonna rip this place apart.